D1406788

ALWAYS SHARE YOUR ICEBERG

A Penguin's Guide to Life

Illustrated by

JAMISON ODONE

TILBURY HOUSE PUBLISHERS, THOMASTON, MAINE

Tilbury House Publishers
12 Starr Street
Thomaston, Maine 04861
800-582-1899
www.tilburyhouse.com

Illustrations © 2017 by Jamison Odone

Hardcover ISBN 978-0-88448-569-8
eBook ISBN 978-9-88448-571-1

First hardcover printing May 2017

15 16 17 18 19 20 XXX 10 9 8 7 6 5 4 3 2 1

Library of Congress Control Number: 2017930359

Designed by Jonathan Friedman, Frame25 Productions

Always Share Your Iceberg was illustrated with a Newton Pens Fountain Pen, a TWSBI Fountain Pen, Holbein Watercolors, and Photoshop colors.

Printed in the USA

THIS BOOK IS
DEDICATED TO
AUNT GEORGIANNE
AND UNCLE PETE –

TWO OF THE
VERY BEST!

The time is always right to do what's right.

—Martin Luther King, Jr.

Forbid us something,
and that thing we desire.

—Geoffrey Chaucer

Humor is laughing at what you haven't got
when you ought to have it.

—Langston Hughes

All truths are easy to understand
once they are discovered;

The point is to
discover them.

—Galileo Galilei

I've had a wonderful time,
	but this wasn't it.

—Groucho Marx

Confidence is going after Moby Dick in a rowboat and taking tartar sauce with you.

—Zig Ziglar

Talent hits a target no one else can hit;
Genius hits a target no
one else can see.

—Arthur Schopenhauer

Any fool can make something complicated.
It takes a genius to make it simple.

—Woody Guthrie

I was street smart,
but unfortunately the street
was Rodeo Drive.

—Carrie Fisher

Granted that I must die, how shall I live? That is the fundamental human question.

—Michael Novak

The brave man is not he who
does not feel afraid, but he
who conquers that fear.

—Nelson Mandela

Each had his past shut in him like
the leaves of a book
known to him by his heart,
and his friends could only read the title.

—Virginia Woolf

It is a tragedy that most of us die
before we have begun to live.

—Erich Fromm

I'm not afraid to die, I just don't
want to be there when it happens.

—Woody Allen

For my part I know nothing with any certainty,
but the sight of the stars makes me dream.

—Vincent van Gogh

An appeaser is one
who feeds a crocodile, hoping
it will eat him last.

—Winston Churchill

Life is either a daring adventure or nothing.

—Helen Keller

We have more possibilities available
in each moment than we realize.

—Thich Nhat Hanh

The only Zen you can find
on the tops of mountains is the
Zen you bring up there.

—Robert M. Pirsig

I experience a period of frightening clarity in those moments when nature is so beautiful.

—Vincent van Gogh

I am prepared to meet my Maker.
Whether my Maker is prepared for the great
ordeal of meeting me is another matter.

—Winston Churchill

All truly great thoughts
are conceived by walking.

—Friedrich Nietzsche

She wasn't doing a thing that I could see,
except standing there, leaning on the
balcony railing, holding the universe together.

—J.D. Salinger

When they go low, we go high.

—Michelle Obama

You are braver than you believe,

stronger than you seem,

and smarter than you think.

—A. A. Milne, from *Pooh's Grand Adventure*

If you wish to make an apple pie from scratch,
you must first invent the universe.

—Carl Sagan

It's no use going back to yesterday
because I was a different person then.

—Lewis Carroll

There are things known and there
are things unknown, and in between
are the doors of perception.

—Aldous Huxley

Earth laughs in flowers.

—Ralph Waldo Emerson

You've got to jump off cliffs all the time
and build your wings on the way down.

—Ray Bradbury

Stand for something or you
will fall for anything.

Today's mighty oak is yesterday's
nut that held its ground.

—Rosa Parks

For most of history,
Anonymous was a woman.

—Virginia Woolf

I had crossed the line. I was free; but there was
no one to welcome me to the land of freedom.
I was a stranger in a strange land.

—Harriet Tubman

When someone shows you who they are,
believe them the first time.

—Maya Angelou

I can resist everything
except temptation.

—Oscar Wilde

There are many ways to be free.
One of them is to transcend reality by
imagination, as I try to do.

—Anais Nin

It was the best of times,
it was the worst of times.

—Charles Dickens

Today you are you! That is truer than true!

There is no one alive who is you-er than you.

—Dr. Seuss

Do not seek death. Death will find you.

But seek the road which

makes death a fulfillment.

—Dag Hammarskjold

Everything has beauty,
but not everyone sees it.

—Confucius

The most dangerous creation of any society
is the man who has nothing to lose.

—James Baldwin

Kiss me and you will see how important I am.

—Sylvia Plath

At the center of the universe dwells
the Great Spirit. And that center is
really everywhere. It is within each of us.

—Black Elk

The only difference between me
and a madman is that I am not mad.

—Salvador Dali

**Glory is fleeting,
but obscurity is forever.**

—Napoleon Bonaparte

Life can only be understood backwards;
but it must be lived forwards.

—Soren Kierkegaard

It always seems impossible until it's done.

—Nelson Mandela

I can calculate the motion of heavenly bodies,
but not the madness of people.

—Isaac Newton

Only two things are infinite,

    the universe and human stupidity,

        and I'm not sure about the former.

—Albert Einstein

Many of life's failures are people
who did not realize how close they
were to success when they gave up.

—Thomas Edison

Don't pray for an easy life, pray for
the strength to endure a difficult one.

—Bruce Lee

It is our choices, Harry, that show what
we truly are, far more than our abilities.

—J. K. Rowling

Sources

1. "The time is always right to do what's right."
Martin Luther King, Jr., 1929–1968, American civil rights activist; from his 1964 Oberlin College speech, "The Future of Integration"

2. "Forbid us something, and that thing we desire."
Geoffrey Chaucer, c. 1343–1400, English poet; from his unfinished *The Canterbury Tales*

3. "Humor is laughing at what you haven't got when you ought to have it."
Langston Hughes, 1902–1967, American writer and social activist; from *The Book of Negro Humor* (1966)

4. "All truths are easy to understand once they are discovered; the point is to discover them."
Galileo Galilei, 1564–1642, Italian astronomer; paraphrased from his 1632 *Dialogue Concerning the Two Chief World Systems*

5. "I've had a wonderful time, but this wasn't it."
Groucho Marx, 1890–1977, American comedian, actor, and movie producer; paraphrased from the 1937 movie *Duck Feathers*

6. "Confidence is going after Moby Dick in a rowboat and taking tartar sauce with you."
Hilary Hinton "Zig" Ziglar, 1926–2012, American author, salesman and motivational speaker; from *Raising Positive Kids in a Negative World* (1985)

7. "Talent hits a target no one else can hit; Genius hits a target no one else can see."
Arthur Schopenhauer, 1788–1860, German philosopher; from *The World as Will and Representation*

8. "Any fool can make something complicated. It takes a genius to make it simple."
Woody Guthrie, 1912–1967, American folk musician; variants of this saying have also been attributed to English economist E. F. Schumacher and Albert Einstein

9. "I was street smart, but unfortunately the street was Rodeo Drive."
Carrie Fisher, 1956–2016, American actress; variant of her 3 January 2016 tweet "I basically consider myself street smart...unfortunately that street is Rodeo Drive."

10. "Granted that I must die, how shall I live? That is the fundamental human question."
Michael Novak, b. 1933, American Catholic philosopher; from *The Experience of Nothingness* (1970)

11. "The brave man is not he who does not feel afraid, but he who conquers that fear."
Nelson Mandela, 1918–2013, South African revolutionary and statesman; from his book *The Long Walk to Freedom* (1995)

12. "Each had his past shut in him like the leaves of a book known to him by his heart, and his friends could only read the title."
Virginia Woolf, 1882–1941, British novelist; from *Jacob's Room* (1922)

13. "It is a tragedy that most of us die before we have begun to live."
Erich Fromm, 1900–1980, German social psychologist and philosopher

14. "I'm not afraid to die, I just don't want to be there when it happens."
Woody Allen, b. 1935, American comic, actor, and auteur; from his book *Without Feathers*, 1975; sometimes misattributed to Spike Milligan

15. "For my part I know nothing with any certainty, but the sight of the stars makes me dream."
Vincent van Gogh, 1853–1890, Dutch painter; paraphrased from a July 1888 letter to his brother Theo

16. "An appeaser is one who feeds a crocodile, hoping it will eat him last."
Winston Churchill, 1874–1965, British statesman; in *Reader's Digest* (December 1954)

17. "Life is either a daring adventure or nothing."
Helen Keller, 1880–1968, American writer and activist; from her book *The Open Door* (1957)

18. "We have more possibilities available in each moment than we realize."
Thich Nhat Hanh, b. 1926, expatriate Vietnamese peace activist and Buddhist monk; quoted by James Miller in *Visions from Earth* (2004)

19. "The only Zen you can find on the tops of mountains is the Zen you bring up there."
Robert M. Pirsig, b. 1928, American philosopher and novelist; from *Zen and the Art of Motorcycle Maintenance* (1974)

20. "I experience a period of frightening clarity in those moments when nature is so beautiful."
Vincent van Gogh, 1853–1890, Dutch painter

21. "I am prepared to meet my Maker. Whether my Maker is prepared for the great ordeal of meeting me is another matter."
Winston Churchill, 1874–1965, British statesman; quoted in the *New York Times Magazine* (1964)

22. "All truly great thoughts are conceived by walking."
Friedrich Nietzsche, 1844–1900, German philosopher; from *Twilight of the Idols* (1889)

23. "She wasn't doing a thing that I could see, except standing there, leaning on the balcony railing, holding the universe together."
J. D. Salinger, 1919–2010, American writer; from his short story "A Girl I Knew" (1948)

24. "When they go low, we go high."
Michelle Obama, b. 1964, American lawyer, writer, and First Lady; speaking at the 2016 Democratic National Convention

25. "You are braver than you believe, stronger than you seem, and smarter than you think."
Uncredited Disney writer of the film *Pooh's Grand Adventure: The Search for Christopher Robin;* the line is commonly misattributed to A. A. Milne, 1882–1956, British author of *Winnie the Pooh*

26. "If you wish to make an apple pie from scratch, you must first invent the universe."
Carl Sagan, 1934–1996, American astronomer; from *Cosmos* (1980)

27. "It's no use going back to yesterday because I was a different person then."
Lewis Carroll, pen name of Charles Lutwidge Dodgson, 1832–1898, British writer and mathematician; from *Alice in Wonderland* (1865)

28. "There are things known and there are things unknown, and in between are the doors of perception."
Aldous Huxley, 1894–1963, British author of *Brave New World* (1932); paraphrased from *The Doors of Perception* (1954)

29. "Earth laughs in flowers."
Ralph Waldo Emerson, 1803–1882, American philosopher, essayist, and poet; from his poem "Hamatreya" (1846)

30. "You've got to jump off cliffs all the time and build your wings on the way down."
Ray Bradbury, 1920–2012, American writer; paraphrased from an interview response on John Blake's *CNN: Living* (August 2, 2010)

31. "Stand for something or you will fall for anything. Today's mighty oak is yesterday's nut that held its ground."
Rosa Parks, 1913–2005, American civil rights activist

32. "For most of history, Anonymous was a woman."
Virginia Woolf, 1882–1941, British novelist; paraphrased from *A Room of One's Own* (1929), where she wrote: "I would venture to guess that Anon, who wrote so many poems without signing them, was often a woman."

33. "I had crossed the line. I was free; but there was no one to welcome me to the land of freedom. I was a stranger in a strange land."
Harriet Tubman, c. 1822–1913, African-American abolitionist, escaped slave, and hero; quoted in Sarah H. Bradford's *Harriet, the Moses of Her People* (1886)

34. "When someone shows you who they are, believe them the first time."
Maya Angelou, 1928–2014, African-American poet, memoirist, and activist; as quoted and paraphrased by Oprah Winfrey on *Oprah's Lifeclass*

35. "I can resist everything except temptation."
Oscar Wilde, 1854–1900, Irish writer; from *Lady Windermere's Fan* (1892), Act 1

36. "There are many ways to be free. One of them is to transcend reality by imagination, as I try to do."
Anais Nin, 1903–1977, French author; from *The Diary of Anais Nin,* Vol. 4 1944–1947

37. "It was the best of times, it was the worst of times."
Charles Dickens, 1812–1870, British novelist; from *A Tale of Two Cities* (1859)

38. "Today you are you! That is truer than true!
There is no one alive who is you-er than you."
Dr. Seuss, pen name of Theodor Seuss Geisel, 1904–1991; from *Happy Birthday to You!* (1959)

39. "Do not seek death. Death will find you. But seek the road which makes death a fulfillment."
Dag Hammarskjöld, 1905–1961, Swedish diplomat and Secretary General of the United Nations; from *Markings* (1964), journal entries published after his death

40. "Everything has beauty, but not everyone sees it."
Confucius, 551–479 BC, Chinese social philosopher

41. "The most dangerous creation of any society is the man who has nothing to lose."
James Baldwin, 1924–1987, American author and social critic; from a 1962 *New Yorker* essay, "Letter from a Region in My Mind," republished in *The Fire Next Time* (1963)

42. "Kiss me and you will see how important I am."
Sylvia Plath, 1932–1963, American writer; from *The Unabridged Journals of Sylvia Plath* (1962)

43. "At the center of the universe dwells the Great Spirit. And that center is really everywhere. It is within each of us."
Nicholas Black Elk, c. 1863–1950, Oglala Lakota spiritual leader; paraphrased from *The Sacred Pipe: Black Elk's Account of the Seven Rites of the Oglala Sioux* (1953), as told to Joseph Epes Brown

44. "The only difference between me and a madman is that I am not mad."
Salvador Dali, 1904–1989, Spanish surrealist artist; quoted in *The Art Digest,* Jan. 1, 1935

45. "Glory is fleeting, but obscurity is forever."
Napoléon Bonaparte, 1769–1821, Emperor of France

46. "Life can only be understood backwards; but it must be lived forwards."
Søren Kierkegaard, 1813–1855, Danish philosopher and theologian; in *The Journals of Soren Kierkegaard, 1840s*

47. "It always seems impossible until it's done."
Nelson Mandela, 1918–2013, South African revolutionary and statesman; quoted in Barack Obama's eulogy for him

48. "I can calculate the motion of heavenly bodies, but not the madness of people."
Isaac Newton, 1643–1727, English scientist who discovered the Laws of Gravity; possibly in response to a question about the South Sea Bubble financial panic; a variant is given in the 1850 *Church of England Quarterly Review*

49. "Only two things are infinite, the universe and human stupidity, and I'm not sure about the former."
Albert Einstein, 1879–1955, theoretical physicist who published the special and general theories of relativity; variant of a disputed quotation first located in 1988

50. "Many of life's failures are people who did not realize how close they were to success when they gave up."
Thomas Alva Edison, 1847–1931, American inventor and businessman; 1877 statement quoted in Deborah Headstrom-Page's *From Telegraph to Light Bulb with Thomas Edison* (2007)

51. "Don't pray for an easy life, pray for the strength to endure a difficult one."
Bruce Lee, 1940–1973, Chinese American martial artist and actor

52. "It is our choices, Harry, that show what we truly are, far more than our abilities."
J. K. Rowling, b. 1965; from *Harry Potter and the Chamber of Secrets* (1999)

JAMISON ODONE is an author and illustrator of children's books and graphic novels as well as an exhibiting artist and professor of illustration at Frostburg State University in Maryland. *Publishers Weekly* said of his 2007 debut book, *Honey Badgers*, "Odone, tapping into a powerful vein of fantasy, has created the kind of book certain children will cling to, years after they abandon the rest of their picture book collections." His books include *The Bedtime Train, Alice's Adventures in Wonderland, Mole Had Everything, Annabel Lee*, and *Poor Joseph*. He writes a blog, "The Stuff Inside Jamison Odone's Head," at www.jamisonodone.wordpress.com, and frequently posts new work at instagram@jamisonodone. Odone lives with his wife and children in Maryland.